Vinnie and Abraham

Vinnie Ream at work upon her Lincoln bust.

Vinnie and Abraham

Dawn FitzGerald
Illustrated by Catherine Stock

ini Charlesbridge

For my daughter, Brynn—D.F.

For Ruth and Rudi Lea—C.S.

Photograph credits:
p. 6: *Vinnie Ream.* Photographer unknown. Biographical file. Prints and Photographs Division. LC-USZ62-10284. Courtesy of the Library of Congress.
p. 43: *Abraham Lincoln,* statue by Vinnie Ream. Courtesy of the Architect of the Capitol. Used by permission.

Published by Charlesbridge
85 Main Street
Watertown, MA 02472
(617) 926-0329
www.charlesbridge.com

Library of Congress Cataloging-in-Publication Data
FitzGerald, Dawn.
    Vinnie and Abraham / Dawn FitzGerald ; illustrated by Catherine Stock.
        p. cm.
    ISBN 978-1-57091-658-8 (reinforced for library use)
1. Ream, Vinnie, 1847-1914. 2. Sculptors—United States—Biography—Juvenile literature. 3. Women sculptors—United States—Biography—Juvenile literature.
4. Lincoln, Abraham, 1809-1865—Portraits—Juvenile literature.
I. Stock, Catherine, ill. II.Title.
NB237.R38F58 2007
730.92—dc22   2006009033

Printed in China
(hc) 10 9 8 7 6 5 4 3 2 1

Illustrations done in watercolor
Display type and text type set in Snell BT and Sabon
Color separations by Chroma Graphics, Singapore
Printed and bound by Regent Publishing Services
Production supervision by Brian G. Walker
Designed by Susan Mallory Sherman

*If you lie down to rest on the green grass, watch the sunlight glisten
and the leaves glow; coax the birds to come and sing to you. . . .
Watch the ants toil and take from their patience. Watch the spider
weave its web and take lessons from its skill. Listen to the thousands
of voices and hear how busy nature is. She does not lose a moment.
She does not tire. Why should we?*

— *Vinnie Ream*

Well-behaved women seldom make history.
— *Laurel Thatcher Ulrich*

"Vinnie Ream, make me a bird."
"Make me a wolf."
"Make my face!"

The children gathered around the curly-haired girl as she scooped up the riverbank clay and molded the figures with her quick hands—a bird, a wolf, and finally the face of the Winnebago Indian girl.

"It looks just like me, Vinnie," she said. And it did, for Vinnie Ream had a gift for sculpture.

Vinnie loved her carefree days in the Wisconsin territory. But when the Civil War began, she and her family moved to Washington, DC. Life in the wartime capital was difficult, and Vinnie's family struggled to make ends meet.

Although she was poor, Vinnie's love for music and art enriched her life. She sang and played her guitar for wounded soldiers in the hospital.

In her coat pocket Vinnie carried a sketchbook and drew pictures of the people and things she saw on the busy Washington streets.

Once, among the crowds, she noticed a tall man in a stovepipe hat and dark suit. She recognized him immediately—President Abraham Lincoln! Vinnie's parents were strong supporters of the president. Vinnie admired his bravery in walking openly among the people during a time of war, when he received death threats daily.

She studied his sad expression and wished she were back home along the riverbanks molding the president's face in clay. She glanced at the mud in the street, tempted to scoop some up and create right then and there. But Vinnie was late for her new job at the U.S. Post Office Department.

Kaboom! Boom!

Startled by the cannon fire echoing from the nearby southern battle line, Vinnie sighed. "I'm late and art will have to wait."

Since so many men had left to become soldiers, some companies were willing to hire women—at reduced wages, of course. Only fourteen years old, Vinnie was one of the first women hired at the post office. She worked in the dead letter office, sorting undeliverable mail, addressed to people who had moved away or died.

All day long Vinnie's nimble fingers sorted hundreds of pieces of mail. Her hands ached. The only thing that made the work bearable was her noon break.

"Where are you rushing off to, Miss Vinnie Ream?" her co-workers asked.

"To visit some grave friends," she replied.

Every day Vinnie ate lunch alone in the Washington graveyards
where she studied and admired the statues above the tombstones.
Touching her weary hands to the cold marble soothed her while
she dreamed of creating her own statues someday.

But like the dead letters she sorted, she was going nowhere.
"I'll have to make my own opportunity if I ever hope to make art."

Determined, Vinnie knocked on the door of a famous Washington sculptor. When Clark Mills answered, he saw a pretty girl with chestnut curls and dark eyes. "Are you here for a modeling job?" he asked.

"No, sir. I'd like to make art."

Clark Mills was amused but curious. He invited Vinnie into his studio and tossed her a lump of clay. Two hours later he inspected her model—the likeness of an Indian chief she once knew.

"You have extraordinary talent," he said. He offered Vinnie a job as an apprentice sculptor. "I want you to start immediately."

Vinnie skipped, danced, and pranced all the way home to tell her parents the wonderful news.

They were not happy. "The post office pays more," they reminded her.

Vinnie would not give up. She persuaded the post office to let her leave work early each day—but only after she processed 200 letters—to study with Clark Mills.

Vinnie worked hard, and word of her talent spread. It wasn't long before congressmen started coming to the studio to have their statues made by Clark Mills's charming apprentice. As they sat before her, puffing themselves up with importance, Vinnie captured their likenesses in clay.

But she had not forgotten the very tall man with the craggy, lined face whom she longed to sculpt more than anyone else.

The congressmen laughed when she told them her wish.

"The president is busy fighting a war," they said.

"What big dreams you have, Miss Ream!" they said.

Vinnie's face flushed red with embarrassment. But she didn't give up. "Sit still, please," she said.

Day after day she sculpted, and day after day she pleaded.

Before long, several congressmen agreed to talk to the president on her behalf. It was not an easy task.

"She's lively and beautiful," the congressmen told the president.

"Vinnie Ream is talented and hard-working," they appealed to him.

But each time Lincoln said no. "Why would anyone want to sculpt such a homely man?" he asked.

The congressmen tried one last time to change his mind. "She's a poor girl—self-taught—raised in a log cabin out west."

That got his attention.

"Poor? Self-taught? Raised in a log cabin? Such a person is not unfamiliar to me," Lincoln said. He finally agreed to sit for Vinnie.

Vinnie couldn't contain her joy. She was just sixteen years old, but she now had a regular appointment with the president: a half hour a day, five days a week, until the sculpture was finished.

Winter turned to spring and the apple blossoms bloomed around Washington, DC. Vinnie visited the White House every day to work on her model of the president. When she spoke to him, he was "Mr. President." But in her head, he was Abraham, her friend. Sometimes they spoke of happy things—their common childhood experiences, or their love for music, art, and books.

Other times, they said nothing at all. Vinnie watched the president mourn the deaths of thousands of soldiers who died fighting the war. She struggled each day to depict Abraham's brave, sad face in clay.

By mid-April, five months after she had begun, Vinnie had captured the president's image. She was delighted.

Throughout the capital there was even more to celebrate. The war was over—the Union was saved! Soldiers returned home to their families, marching bands played in the streets, and people began to hope that life would be good again.

But Vinnie's—and the nation's—joy wouldn't last long. On April 14, 1865, during a play at Ford's Theatre, President Lincoln was shot and killed by a man named John Wilkes Booth.

Vinnie was devastated. She stood among the weeping crowd at the railroad station to say a final goodbye to the president, her beloved friend, Abraham.

The newspapers reported that Congress wanted to hire a sculptor to create a memorial statue of President Lincoln. Vinnie wrote a letter asking for the job.

The congressmen said, "This isn't a job for a mere girl. This is a job for a great American sculptor."

"I was meant to create this statue," Vinnie pleaded. Some of the congressmen whom she had sculpted persuaded the others to let her present her case before the Congress.

"What training do you have in art?" boomed a senator from the East.

Vinnie swallowed hard. "I taught myself, mostly."

Another scolded, "You, Miss Ream, exhibit a most unladylike persistence!"

Vinnie left the chamber with her head bowed and tears in her eyes. She was sure she had lost her chance to sculpt the Lincoln statue.

But Vinnie's talent could not be ignored. While many famous male sculptors portrayed Lincoln as a warrior king or saint, Vinnie's model simply showed the president as the kind and gentle man she knew. When the vote was called, there were nine "nays" and twenty-three "yeas." Vinnie Ream had won! She was the youngest artist and the first woman to receive a commission from the U.S. government.

Vinnie got right to work. She set up her studio in the Capitol building, filling it with art supplies, flowers, and the soft cooing of her pet turtledoves.

And Vinnie added one more thing—something no other artist had ever done before. She opened her studio to the public. Every day, citizens, congressmen, and soldiers—many of whom had fought for "Father Abraham"—filed through the studio to watch the tiny young sculptress, perched on a scaffold, shaping the giant model, which at nearly seven feet tall was slightly larger than Lincoln's six-foot-four-inch frame.

Although Vinnie's studio was always open, some people's minds were very much closed against her.

Critics tried to discourage her. "This statue can't be made," they said. "She's only a girl and is sure to fail." Day after day they ridiculed her artistic ability, her youth, and her gender.

The public hoped that their tax dollars would not be wasted on this young girl. Vinnie only worked harder—until at last, her Lincoln model was complete.

But Vinnie still wasn't finished. The model was clay and plaster, but the statue had to be marble. Vinnie loaded her life-sized model, her doves, and her guitar on board the ship *Dana* and set sail from New York Harbor to Italy to turn the model into stone.

Italian artists were curious to meet the daring American sculptress who had competed with men and won. Vinnie visited the finest quarries of Carrara and learned the secret to finding the whitest marble. "Late at night, after it rains," they told her, "hold a candle beside the glistening stones and choose the one that glows like *la luna*—the moon!"

She approached the task of sculpting the expensive marble with reverence and care. Carving the marble took nearly a year, with the help of the finest Italian artisans.

Five years after she received her commission, Vinnie's statue of Abraham Lincoln stood draped in a silk American flag in the Capitol rotunda, waiting for the public unveiling. The Marine Band played as hundreds of people gathered around the platform to see if the young sculptress had succeeded or failed.

Vinnie stood among the crowd, but at barely five feet tall, she could not see her statue. It didn't matter. She closed her eyes, and in her mind she could see every detail of his expression, every fold of his cape, every curve of his hands.

In the hushed silence, Vinnie was sure the crowd could hear her heart pounding in hope and fear for what this moment would bring. Would her work find acceptance and respect, or only scorn and shame?

President Grant gave the signal, and slowly the Stars and Stripes slipped off the polished marble.

A few people gasped.

An old soldier quietly wept.

A former slave clapped her hands together.

Soon thunderous applause echoed through the Capitol halls.

For there stood Vinnie's statue of Abraham Lincoln, the sixteenth president of the United States, his head humbly bowed and his hand holding out the Emancipation Proclamation.

The crowd cheered and called for Vinnie to speak. Through her glad tears she smiled and waved, but she was too overcome to say a word. In the end her work spoke for itself. Vinnie Ream had captured her friend Abraham Lincoln in stone, just as Abraham had captured the heart of his country.

A Note from the Author

Much of the dialogue in this story was invented, but the events of the story are true, drawn from the work of Vinnie's biographers and her own writings, too. Vinnie Ream's statue of Abraham Lincoln still stands today in the Capitol rotunda in Washington, DC. After the Lincoln statue, Vinnie created many statues of renowned Americans, including presidents James Garfield and Ulysses S. Grant, as well as General Robert E. Lee.

The Civil War gave American women the opportunity to overcome the Victorian attitudes of the time that discouraged their independence. Many women served as nurses, a few donned men's uniforms and passed as soldiers, and some, like Susan B. Anthony and Elizabeth Cady Stanton, were in the middle of their long struggle to secure a woman's right to vote.

With so many men called away to fight, women replaced them in the work force, which made Vinnie's clerking position at the post office possible. She would have been thrilled to know that in 1980 her first employer, now the United States Postal Service, issued a stamp honoring her artistic achievement.

After her success with the Lincoln statue, Vinnie received numerous marriage proposals, but she refused them to devote herself to her art. In 1878, when she was 30 years old, she married Lieutenant Richard Leveridge Hoxie. She later gave birth to a son, Richard Ream Hoxie, in 1883.

Her husband asked her to give up her work in order to devote herself entirely to her family, and she did—for a while. But she could not give it up forever. "My work has never been labor, but an ecstatic delight to my soul. I have worked in my studio not envying kings in their splendor; my mind to me was my kingdom, and my work more than diamonds and rubies. If my encouraging words can help any struggling artist to have new hope, I shall be glad. We know that we can only portray what is in us. . . . What we give is what we have: Our work speaks for us." In 1906 Vinnie returned to work, with a commission to sculpt Iowa governor Samuel Kirkwood.

Vinnie completed her last sculpture as she was dying of kidney failure. She was so weak that her husband rigged a hoist and pulley with a boatswain's chair so she could reach all areas of her work while sitting down. This sculpture was the first free-standing statue of Sequoyah, the creator of the Cherokee alphabet, which is also displayed in the Capitol. Vinnie thought it fitting that her first and last creations were of Native Americans.

Vinnie died in 1914 at age 67. She was buried at Arlington National Cemetery beneath a statue she designed of Sappho, a Greek poet who also dared to rebel against the conventions of her time to create art.

Abraham Lincoln, statue by Vinnie Ream.

Resources

Arlington National Cemetery
www.arlingtoncemetery.net/vrhoxie.htm
Contains descriptions of how Vinnie Ream lived in Italy and turned the statue into marble, pictures of the Sequoyah statue in the U.S. Capitol building, and pictures of Vinnie's gravesite with the statue she designed of the Greek poet, Sappho.

Coleman, Penny. *Girls: A History of Growing Up Female in America*. New York: Scholastic, Inc., 2000.

Cooper, Edward S. *Vinnie Ream: An American Sculptor*. Chicago: Academy Chicago Publishers, 2004.

Hoose, Phillip. *We Were There, Too! Young People in U.S. History*. New York: Farrar, Straus and Giroux, 2001.

Langley Hall, Gordon. *Vinnie Ream: The Story of the Girl Who Sculpted Lincoln*. New York: Holt, Rinehart and Winston, 1963.

Sherwood, Glenn V. *A Labor of Love: The Life & Art of Vinnie Ream*. Hygiene, Colorado: SunShine Press Publications, 1997.

Vinnie Ream Home Page
www.vinnieream.com/
Contains excerpts from her speeches and photos of Vinnie and her work, including the Lincoln statue; newspaper and magazine articles describing the Lincoln statue's unveiling and Vinnie's presentation before Congress; and a picture of the 1980 Vinnie Ream stamp.